Stanley & District
THEN & NOW

RON HINDHAUGH

COUNTY DURHAM BOOKS

The compilers of this book have endeavoured to contact and seek permission from the copyright holders of all the photographs used herein. If we have inadvertently used a picture without permission we would be grateful if the copyright holder would contact us so that we can make the proper acknowledgement in any future editions.

Published by County Durham Books, 2006

County Durham Books is the imprint of Durham County Council

ISBN 189758587X

Stanley & District
THEN & NOW

The hardest part about doing a 'Then and Now' book, especially one of this size, is choosing which pictures to put in and which pictures to leave out.

Stanley has changed a great deal over the years and more changes are planned. The old bus station which opened in 1974 was demolished in 2005 and a new one has been built on the site of Mary Street car park. Further work is planned to link this new bus station to the front street. A 25 metre pool and a leisure pool have been added to the Louisa Sports Centre replacing the Burns Leisure Pool (Stanley Baths) which was demolished in 1997. A new medical centre is to be built to replace the current one which is to be demolished.

The area surrounding Stanley has also changed considerably. The collieries that once dominated the landscape, as well as the local economy, have long gone, replaced with housing and industrial estates. Old railway lines that served these collieries are now public footpaths or cycle paths that, in some cases, allow people to travel from one side of the county to the other.

I have recorded some of these changes on 35mm film and digital media, so who knows in fifty or so years time someone else could be doing another 'Then and Now' book.

Where possible I have tried to show the areas of greatest change from the same position, which was not always easy owing to the greater volume of traffic today. I have also included some pictures where change is not quite so apparent.

All of the 'Now' pictures were taken during 2006 and as I mentioned earlier, change is on the way so watch this space.

Many thanks must go to all the people who have helped me in various ways while I have been compiling this book.

Ron Hindhaugh, 2006

WEST ROAD. ANNFIELD PLAIN.   1205

In 1820 Annfield Plain was a small hamlet consisting of a single street named Ravensworth Road with an offshoot called Red Row. This is now West Road. On the right is the Coach and Horses. One licensee, Robert Freick, had a race horse which, when it died, had its head, complete with bridle stuffed, mounted and hung behind the bar for many years. It was known as Freick's Billy.

The Coach and Horses was demolished and rebuilt in the mid 1960's. Further development has taken place on the right of the road though little has changed to the left.

FRONT STREET, ANNFIELD PLAIN.

10453.

An early view of Front Street. The Co-op, which can be seen on the right, was built in 1873. A glass veranda was added later but this was demolished in 1925 when a new set of shops were built.

Current day Front Street looks a lot different. The Co-op closed in the early 1970's and the buildings were demolished to make way in 1998 for Manor House Residential Home. Part of the Central Buildings of the store was rebuilt brick by brick as an attraction at Beamish Open Air Museum

Front Street looking towards the railway. The ornate iron structure on the left is an underground toilet which opened in 1907. The Queen's Head Hotel, on the right, was originally a long low double fronted building with a large sign on the front which read "Queen's Head Hotel John Dodd Wine and Spirit Merchant Good Stabling".

The underground toilet was closed in 1917 after a gentleman called Mr. Mumford fell down the steps and was killed. The mini roundabout now marks its approximate location. In 1901 The Queens Head Hotel was rebuilt into the building we see today.

West Road. Here we see H. Niklas Pork Butcher and Hunters who sold "good tea and good butter". Hunters also had a store in Stanley. Further on beyond the boot store is the Co-op building. On the right of the picture is H & M Atkinson Fish Merchant.

Hunters, Niklas and the Co-op have long since departed. The building we see in their place is Manor House Residential Home. The shop which was H & M Atkinson Fish Merchant is now Golden Fry fish and chip shop.

Catchgate, Annfield Plain.

The first Wesleyan Church was opened on 9th May 1854 and was later rebuilt and enlarged. It was damaged by mining subsidence and a third church was built and opened in 1870. As the population of Annfield Plain grew a new and larger church was needed. The church in this picture opened in June 1900.

St John's Methodist Church, as it became known in 1932, closed for public worship in 1963. As you can see, bungalows have since been built on the spot where the church stood.

The Three Horse Shoes is known to have been in existence as early as 1828. It is said, however, that Oliver Cromwell visited the Three Horse Shoes in the 1640's. One suggestion for the name of the inn is derived from its sign which represents the arms of a blacksmith or farrier who were sometimes publicans. Another suggestion is that it came from a game similar to quoits but played with three horse shoes.

As you can see, this popular pub at Maiden Law, which licensee Joanne Cordey took over in September 2005, has been extended and modernised over the years.

THEN

Shield Row

This picture of Shield Row was taken from the old railway bridge. Rodham Terrace and Gordon Terrace can be seen on the left. Station Houses and Railway Street are on the right.

This picture was taken from the new footbridge. Railway Street and Station Houses have long gone and on once open fields, more housing, including Clark Street, has been built.

STATION ROAD   STANLEY.   No. II.

Circa 1910, and here we see a view down Station Road. South Thorn and Gordon Terrace are on the right. The old railway bridge mentioned on page 13 is just about visible at the very bottom of the road.

South Thorn and Gordon Terrace have not changed, but the old railway bridge was demolished on the 15th October 2005. A new, very large, footbridge has now been built in its place.

The Blue Bell is known to have existed in 1851 when it was known as a Jerry (a public house which only had a licence to sell beer) and described as a rough and ready pub with stone flagged floors and low ceilings.

It is no longer rough and ready and has been extended into the popular pub you see today by the present landlord Eddie Hall, who has been the licensee since February 1999. This very popular pub is furnished with the world famous "mouse furniture" by Robert Thompson of Kilburn, North Yorkshire.

SOUTH MOOR. 12309

The West Craghead Colliery, on the left, was sunk in 1839 by William Hedley. When the Louisa Colliery opened in 1863 this pit closed only to be reopened in 1898 by the South Moor Collieries Ltd and renamed the William Pit after the then owner William Hedley junior. The colliery was always known locally as the Billy Pit and the community of Old South Moor grew around it.

The Billy Pit eventually closed and was demolished. The site stood derelict for many years until the houses on the left were built. On the right is Wilgrow Nursery which was established in 1988.

FRONT STREET, SOUTH MOOR.

South Moor Co-op was opened as a branch of the West Stanley Co-op on the 18th August 1900. A procession of Co-op horses and vehicles took place on opening day and tea was given in a marquee on the store fields. A concert was also held in the Co-op hall at Stanley.

At the end of 1996 contractors started to demolish the old building to make way for new flats. Hedley House, as the flats are named, opened in 1997.

The old colliery offices at the Billy pit were closed in 1906 when these offices were built. They incorporated the colliery manager's house 'The Limes', which was the first house in South Moor to have a bathroom.

After the offices were demolished the site stood empty for a number of years. Work started on these bungalows at the beginning of 2004 with the residents moving in shortly after.

MAIN STREET, SOUTH MOOR (895)

Most of the shops in this picture were built at the beginning of the twentieth century. Names such as Matthew Martin and Mr Bainbridge would have been familiar to the people of South Moor.

The name on the shop fronts and the things they sell may have changed but very little else has.

THEN

SOUTH MOOR. (581)

Mr. Thomas Oxley opened the South Moor Hotel, on the right, on the 10th December 1897. He had originally owned the Oak Inn at Old South Moor but as the population increased in New South Moor he transferred the licence to this pub. In the empty space beyond the Hotel would be built the Arcadia Cinema which opened on the 24th March 1914.

The Hotel was burnt out in 2005 and as I write is up for let. The Arcadia Cinema closed in 1962 but the building is still there and is now Little Acorns nursery.

THEN

OXHILL, STANLEY. 902.

The first bridge built here, for the Stanhope and Tyne Railway in 1833, was made of stone. This stone bridge was replaced in 1844 by a girder bridge and at some point in history the area became known as The Arch.

The girder bridge was demolished in 1964 but the area is still known today as The Arch.

High Street, Stanley.

High Street. The Pavilion Cinema opened in April 1923. Next door is St Andrew's Church Institute which was opened on the 9th July 1894.

The Pavilion closed in 1966. G.D. Auto's used the lower part of the building as a car accessory shop and, for a short time, the upper part was an Italian restaurant. The building was demolished in 2001 and the Co-operative Funeral Service was opened the following year.

STANLEY.

This was the first public house to be built in Stanley and opened around 1860. The Stanley Inn, better known as Paddy Rock's, was built on the site of a corve making yard (a corve was a large willow basket used to carry coal in the local pits). The pub was later extended and refurbished. It had two shops attached, one a butchers the other a greengrocers which also held Stanley's first Post Office.

Like most of the buildings in High Street, Paddy Rock's was demolished at the beginning of the 1970's to make way for the town centre bypass.

STATION RD STANLEY.

Station Road. The Theatre Royal in Stanley opened in 1903 but lasted only 27 years before it was destroyed by a fire.

The large covered bus stop which for a long time stood on the site of the old Theatre Royal was demolished in 2002. Further down the road is the old Market Hall which was opened in 1924. It is now Stanley Market Hall Carpet Centre.

Front Street. The Victoria Theatre opened on 29th June 1893. It was originally intended as a public house but could not get a licence. Gracie Fields, Bud Flanagan and Charlie Chaplin are all said to have appeared on stage here. The Victoria Club was formed in the cellar of the building. The old theatre was demolished and the Victoria Cinema opened in 1935, becoming the Essoldo Cinema in 1948 and the Classic Cinema in 1970.

The Classic Cinema closed in 1976 and the building stood empty until it was demolished at the beginning of 1999. Havanna Court flats now stand on the site. The first residents of these flats moved in at the end of February 2000.

WESLEYAN CHAPEL. FRONT ST. STANLEY.

The first Chapel stood on the site of the present council offices. It moved to the site in this picture in 1890 but was found to be too small. The building seen here was built in 1899.

The Chapel was demolished at the end of 1983. The Job Centre which opened in November 1994 is built on the site.

The Commercial, known locally as the Middle House, was known to have been in existence as early as 1873. In around 1940 an upstairs lounge was opened.

Boots Pharmacy, which opened in the mid 1970s, and Carlyons, a florist shop, now occupy the site of the old Commercial.

FRONT STREET, STANLEY   (8)

Remember when traffic was allowed on Stanley Front Street? On the left is the Queens Hotel built in 1898 which stood on the site of Chaytor's Buildings.

The Queens Hotel was demolished in 1971 and £stretcher now stands on the site. In around 1974 the front street was made pedestrian only and now a thriving market takes place every Thursday and Saturday on a street once busy with traffic.

The Louisa Stanley.

Louisa Terrace, on the left, was built in 1867 to house the workers of the Louisa Colliery. However, these houses were found to be too small so larger ones were built in 1894. The Louisa Colliery, which was sunk in 1863, is at the end of the street and was named after the wife of William Bell, who along with William Hedley owned the pit. Later, a second shaft named the Shield Row or New Louisa shaft, was sunk.

The Louisa Colliery closed in 1964. Fine Fare Limited, later to become Asda, opened a store at the bottom of Stanley Front Street in 1961. When larger premises were needed they moved to this 5,800 square metre site in 1977. The building is also home to an eight rink indoor bowling green which is above the store.

8 The Winding Road n⁴ Tanfield Stanley M.L.M.

This is the road from Tantobie to Tanfield c1910.

The housing estate of 'Sleepy Valley' was built in the mid 1930's. A little closer to Tantobie an estate of pre-fabricated houses, or pre-fabs as they were known, was built shortly after the 1939-45 war. This estate was demolished in the 1960s.

THE HOSPITAL . TANFIELD

In 1901-02 an isolation hospital, which had beds for 32 patients, was built at Tanfield by the Lanchester Joint Hospital Board at a cost of around £7,000.

The hospital closed in 1946 and the building was taken over by a clothing manufacturer. The present owner, Mr. Dave Tate, set up a hire firm in the buildings in 1977. Mr. Tate now runs DJ Autogas 4x4 Ltd from the premises.

On the left is Tanfield National School which opened in 1844 and later became known as the Board School. Further down on the same side we come to Front Street and on the right Maude Terrace.

The school was demolished in the 1960's. Later, St Margaret's Drive was built on the site. Hawthorn Terrace, on the right, was a short row of thatched cottages until the present ones were built.

TANFIELD

The Pack Horse, on the left, dates back to as early as 1775. However, the pub could be even older as it is said that Oliver Cromwell, who was born in 1599 and died in 1658, was entertained here. In between Front Street and The Pack Horse is the blacksmith's shop where, it is said, the gates for Tanfield Hall were made.

In the 1980's the Pack Horse was renamed The Sea Horse. Fortunately it reverted back to its old name in the 1990's.

The Rev Thomas Hewan Archdale M.A. of Trinity Collage Dublin was the occupant of the vicarage at Tanfield in 1877.

Old Rectory Close is the name given to the bungalows that now occupy the site. As you can see the view that the old photographer recorded is now nearly obscured by trees.

County Durham Books is the 'publishing wing' of Durham County Council. It designs and publishes a range of books with a connection to County Durham's local history, authors and communities. These are sold in libraries, through retailers across the country, and also by direct sale around the world (including on-line through the online shop).

County Durham Books also operates the sale of other local history books, gifts, stationery and merchandise through Durham County Council's libraries.

You can view and buy our publications on-line wherever you are by visiting www.durham.gov.uk/countydurhambooks

COUNTY DURHAM BOOKS